THIS WALKER BOOK BELONGS TO:

_____

_____

_____

_____

The Blacksmith's

The School

The Wash-house

The Bakery

The Village Green

Tabitha Tripp lives here

Mr Flowerbutts' Garden

Mr Arkwright's House and Bicycle Shed →

To the Swimming Pond ↑

Farmer Parsnip's Farm

Dr Potts' House

This is where Lily Binns and Elsie Crumb live

Farmer Trotter's Farm

Mr Penniman's Shop

The Scarecrow ——→

Mr Tompion's Shop

Podgson's General Store

The Skating Pond ↘

First published 1988 by
Walker Books Ltd
87 Vauxhall Walk
London SE11 5HJ

This edition published 1990

2 4 6 8 10 9 7 5 3

Text © 1988 John Yeoman
Illustrations © 1988 Quentin Blake

Printed in Hong Kong

British Library Cataloguing in Publication Data
A catalogue record for this book is
available from the British Library.

ISBN 0-7445-1371-5

Poems by
John Yeoman

OUR
VILLAGE

Pictures by
Quentin Blake

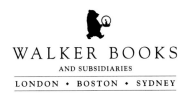

WALKER BOOKS
AND SUBSIDIARIES
LONDON • BOSTON • SYDNEY

Down in the bakery,
His oven glowing bright,
Mr Crumb the baker has been
Working half the night.

Down in the bakery,
While you were safe in bed,
Mr Crumb the baker has been
Busy with his bread.

Round loaves, tall loaves,
Lots and lots and lots,
Some as long as walking-sticks,
And some tied up in knots.

Out from the bakery,
And blinking in the sun,
Mr Crumb the baker's got his
Day's work done.

Every day at eight o'clock
The village people stand and wait,
Some lean upon the window-sill,
And some lean on the garden gate.

When Mr Puce the postman comes
Their anxious faces seem to say,
"I hope he's going to call on me;
I hope I get some post today."

He dips his hand into his sack —
There's something there for one and all;
To some he hands out shopping bills,
And some get letters, large or small.

The lucky ones, just once a year,
Get bulging parcels, tied in yards
Of coloured string with cheerful bows,
And heaps and heaps of birthday cards!

Rattle, rattle, clatter —
Bet you anything you like
It's Mr Henry Arkwright
On his penny-farthing bike.

The front wheel's got the wobbles
And the saddle's got the shakes,
And he honks upon the horn because
He hasn't any brakes.

Though the handlebars are wonky
And the pedals may have rust,
Still Mr Arkwright cycles on
Through clouds and clouds of dust.

Little Miss Thynne gets to school bright and early
To write on the blackboard and put out the slates.
She stands at the window and watches the children
Come scampering in through the wide-open gates.

Little Miss Thynne gives a smile of approval
To see their fresh faces, their neat shoes and socks,
Their smartly brushed hair and their bright caps and bonnets,
Their clean linen shirts and their well-laundered frocks.

Little Miss Thynne never ceases to wonder
How all of the children, in so little time,
Get scruffy and tattered and creased and bedraggled,
And spattered with ink stains and covered in grime.

He stands upon his single leg,
His body stuffed with hay,
And holds his gloved hands wide apart
To scare the birds away.

A battered hat upon his head,
A carrot for a nose,
He might fool me, he might fool you—
But he doesn't fool the crows.

Lily Binns and Elsie Crumb,
Very deaf and rather slow,
Walk together side by side,
Talking everywhere they go.

Flowery hats and bulging handbags,
See them on their daily walk;
Always shuffling arm in arm, and
Everywhere they go they talk.

What they're saying doesn't matter;
Neither of them seems to care.
Lily Binns and Elsie Crumb,
Talking, talking everywhere.

At the wash-house by the river
    you will find Selina Scrubb,
With her bar of soap and scrubbing-brush
    and bubble-covered tub.
She washes socks and skirts and shirts
    and scarves and stockings too,
And she splashes and she sploshes
    till she's soaking through and through.

She rinses them, she wrings them,
    and she puts them in a pile,
And puts the whole lot on her head,
    and gives a little smile
As she trots out to the meadow
    and—most marvellous of sights—
Pegs the washing up to dry,
    like brightly coloured kites.

Dotty Lou is absent-minded,
Never knows the time of day,
Doesn't watch where she is going,
Always seems to lose her way.

Primrose, Patience, Lucy, Dora,
Mopsa, Bella, Annie, Prue,
Marigold and Arabella
Keep an eye on Dotty Lou.

They take her to the fields each morning,
Watch to see that she's all right,
Stop her tumbling in the river,
Bring her home again each night.

Yes, Primrose, Patience, Lucy, Dora,
Mopsa, Bella, Annie, Prue,
Marigold and Arabella
Keep an eye on Dotty Lou.

Mr Samuel Flowerbutts
Is the smallest man I know,
But whatever's in his garden
Seems to grow and grow and grow.

You can sit upon his marrows,
You can clamber through his greens,
And it's possible to lose yourself
Among his runner beans.

His onions are like footballs,
And his turnips are a size,
And his hollyhocks are sprouting up
As if to reach the skies.

Yes, whatever's in his garden
Seems to grow and grow and grow,
Yet Mr Samuel Flowerbutts
Is the smallest man I know.

On a lovely day in summer
When all around is still,
You can hear the noise of laughter
From the pond behind the hill.

The children dive and splash about
With shouts and cries and squeals,
And twist and turn and tumble
Like a lot of slippery eels.

The drinking cattle wonder why
They never go away,
And leave the pond in peace upon
A lovely summer's day.

Butterfly nets and jars and baskets,
Out to the woods and fields we troop—
Eager members of our village
Local natural history group.

Scrambling through the prickly gorses,
Wading in mud up to our knees,
Chasing butterflies, hunting beetles,
Finding fox-holes, climbing trees.

Stings and bites and bumps and scratches,
Back from the woods and fields we troop—
Weary members of our village
Local natural history group.

The Podgsons run the General Store;
It's stacked full of delights:
They've copper pans and waterproofs
And eiderdowns and kites
And walking-sticks and garden brooms
And sacks of flour and rice
And drawing-books and curling tongs
And glue and chocolate mice
And tins of paint and peppercorns
And different kinds of fruit
And cooking oil, and also one
Elastic-sided boot.

And yet it takes you half an hour
To buy a ball of string:
They've got so much in stock that they
Can never find a thing!

Old Farmer Trotter has five pigs,
All fat and pink and white;
He scratches at their backs until
They're grunting with delight.

While Farmer Parsnip ploughs and sows
And reaps and mows and digs,
Old Farmer Trotter's tickling
His five contented pigs.

Scratches, cuts or
Lots and lots
Of nasty
Itchy-itchy spots,

Headache, nosebleed,
Cough or 'flu—
Dr Potts
Knows what to do:

Yellow medicine
Twice a day;
Aches and pains
Soon go away.

Mr Penniman, the tailor,
Snips and sews from morn till night;
Bows and buttons, hems and pockets,
Everything must be just right.

Mr Penniman, the tailor,
Works from morn till night to please;
(Hasn't time to notice he's got
Ragged elbows, threadbare knees).

Tom was given Mr Fluff,
The baby owl, for him to keep;
But all day long while Tom's awake
You'll find that Mr Fluff's asleep.

Tom didn't know what funny kind
Of pet young Mr Fluff would make;
For all night long while Tom's asleep
You'll find that Mr Fluff's awake.

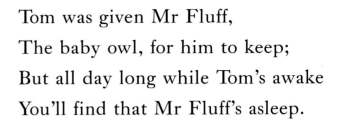

The hurdy gurdy's playing,
All the people run and stare,
For it's Mr Mandolini
And his dancing bear.

You've seen them on the village green,
You've seen them at the fair—
Old Mr Mandolini
And his dancing bear.

The grown-ups rock with laughter
But the children are aware
That there's really nothing sadder
Than a dancing bear.

People passing in the street
Will often find the time to stop
And listen to the tick-a-tock
From Mr Tompion's jeweller's shop.

But once an hour the ticking shop
Becomes as noisy as a zoo:
Whirr, click, bong, bong,
Ding, dong, cuc-KOO, cuc-KOO!

Tabitha Tripp has a house full of pussies—
Pussies that live there or stay for a night—
Tabitha calls them and holds them and strokes them,
Arching her back with a look of delight.

Ginger cats, tortoiseshells, Persians and tabbies,
Playing with cotton-reels, pouncing on flies,
Tabitha sits there and watches them closely,
Purring with pleasure and closing her eyes.

Night comes and Tabitha's counting the pussies—
Counting them over as you count up sheep—
Smoothing her hair with the backs of her fingers,
Curling up gently, and falling asleep.

When the darkness falls and the air grows chill
And the lights go out in the village store,
Then a crowd of folk always makes its way
To the flickering glow from the blacksmith's door

To see Mr Smutts and his red-faced twins
Beat the white-hot iron till the sparks fly high,
As they shape a shoe for the farmer's horse,
Or they mend a gate for the pigman's sty,

Or they fix a blade on a broken skate,
Or they make a bell for a goat or cow.
And they sing and sweat in the smoke and flames,
And the audience claps as they take their bow.

Did you know that the pond at the end of the lane
Has a coating of ice like a great window-pane?
We'll put our thick scarves on and go out to skate
With twistings and turnings and figures of eight.

The water is frozen, the willows are bare,

There's a tingly-tingly nip in the air;

We've put our warm gloves on and come out to skate

With twistings and turnings and figures of eight.

The ice is reflecting the light of the moon;
It's getting quite late now—we must be home soon;
We've lit up the lanterns to have one last skate
With twistings and turnings and figures of eight.

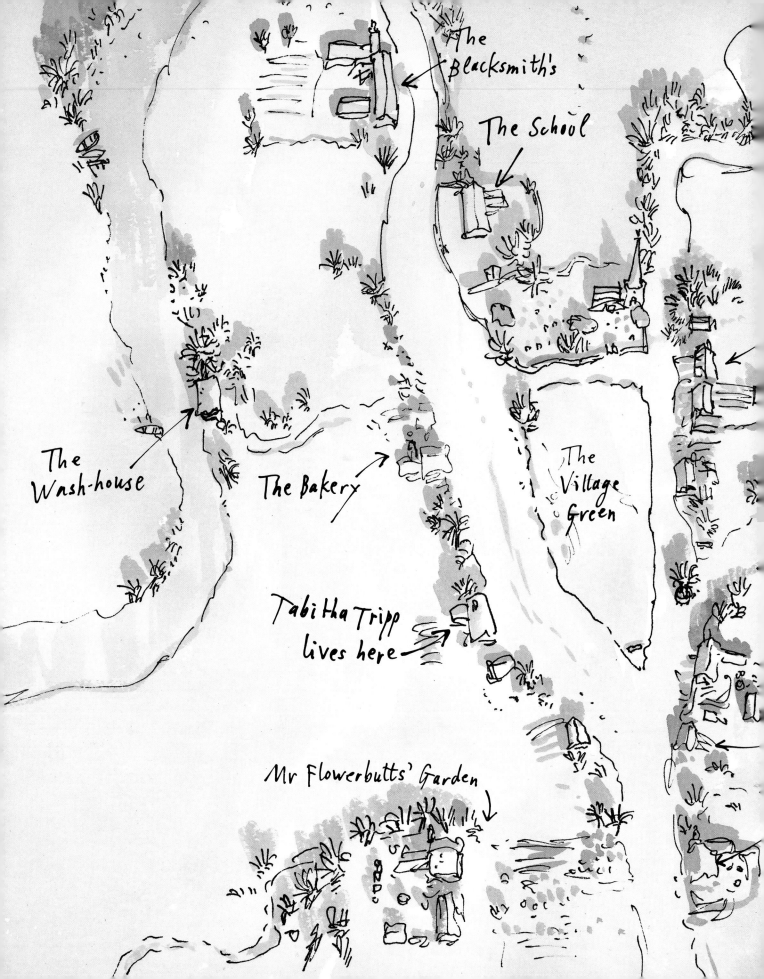

The Blacksmith's

The School

The Wash-house

The Bakery

Tabitha Tripp lives here

The Village Green

Mr Flowerbutts' Garden

Mr Arkwright's
House
and Bicycle
Shed

To the Swimming Pond ↑

Farmer
Parsnip's Farm

Dr Potts'
House

This is where
Lily Binns and
Elsie Crumb
live

Farmer Trotter's
Farm

The Scarecrow ⟶

Mr
Penniman's
Shop

Tompion's
hop

The
Skating
Pond

Podgson's
General Store

MORE WALKER PAPERBACKS
For You to Enjoy

SCRAPBOOKS
by Michael Rosen / Quentin Blake

Four books, each with a different theme, packed with jokes, jingles, poems, silly sayings, crazy conversations and wonderful pictures.

"Great stuff, so long as you don't mind uncontrollable giggles." *The Irish Times*

Under the Bed   0-7445-7763-2
Smelly Jelly Smelly Fish   0-7445-7766-7
Hard-boiled Legs   0-7445-7764-0
Spollyollydiddlytiddlyitis   0-7445-7765-9

£4.50 each

THERE'S AN AWFUL LOT OF WEIRDOS
IN OUR NEIGHBOURHOOD
by Colin McNaughton

Ninety-six rollicking pages of silly verse and pictures – full of the most extraordinary characters you're never likely to meet!

"The book of the year for 7 to 10-year-olds." *The Daily Mail*

0-7445-7778-0   £7.99

THE MAGIC BICYCLE
by Brian Patten / Arthur Robins

When young Danny Harris knocks a witch into a ditch, she puts a spell on his bike that sends him off on an amazing journey around the world!

"Packed with jokes and buzzing with life." *The Mail on Sunday*

0-7445-3651-0   £4.99